The Best Book of

Spaceships

Ian Graham

KINGFISHER

NEW YORK

Author: Ian Graham
Managing Editor: Camilla Hallinan
Series Editor: Sue Nicholson
Illustrators: Gary Bines,
  Lee Gibbons, Ceri Llewellyn
Art Editor: Ch'en-Ling
Art Director and cover design:
  Terry Woodley
Series Designer: Ben White
Production Controller: Kelly Johnson

Photographs on p26 by Martin
  Redfern/NASA

KINGFISHER
Larousse Kingfisher Chambers Inc.
95 Madison Avenue
New York, New York 10016

First published in 1998
10 9 8 7 6 5 4 3 2 1
Copyright © Kingfisher Publications Plc 1998

LIBRARY OF CONGRESS CATALOGING-IN-PUBLICATION DATA
Graham, Ian.
    The best book of spaceships / Ian Graham.—1st ed.
        p.   cm.
    Summary: Illustrations and text describe how humans
have tried to learn more about space and some of the
equipment and vehicles used to do this.
    1. Space vehicles—Juvenile literature. [I. Outer space—
Exploration. 2. Space vehicles.]   I. Title.
TL793.G688   1998
629.47—dc21   97-51599   CIP AC

ISBN 0-7534-5133-6
Printed in Hong Kong

Contents

Looking into space

For thousands of years, people have gazed in wonder at the night sky. Slowly, they learned more and more about the twinkling stars and the planets above them. Many dreamed of visiting and exploring the planets, but there was no way of traveling there. Instead, people had to make do with fuzzy views seen through telescopes.

Nowadays, we have all kinds of spacecraft that can travel into space, visit the planets, and even land on them.

Pathfinder explorer on Mars

Robot explorers

Robot explorers have become our eyes and ears on distant worlds we have not yet visited ourselves.

What's in space?

The Earth is one of nine planets that fly through space around the Sun. The path each planet follows as it flies around the Sun is called an orbit. The Earth takes a year to orbit the Sun once. The Sun is enormous. A million Earths could fit inside it with lots of room to spare.

The pull of gravity

Gravity is an invisible force that pulls things toward it. The Sun is so big, its pull of gravity is strong enough to hold all the planets in their orbits.

Stars
The Sun and stars we can see from Earth are part of a huge group, or galaxy, called the Milky Way

Earth's moon

Mercury
The closest planet to the Sun

The Sun
The star at the center of our Solar System

Earth
Our home planet

Venus
A boiling hot planet where it rains acid

Asteroids
Lumps of rock orbiting the Sun

Mars
A red and rocky planet

Jupiter
The biggest planet in the Solar System

The Solar System

The Solar System is the name given to the Sun's family. It includes the planets and their moons, comets, and all the lumps of rock, dust, and ice that orbit the Sun.

Staging

A rocket is made up of parts called stages. When each stage has used up its fuel, it is dropped to save weight. The rest of the rocket goes on into space.

Spacecraft

The top of the rocket then opens, and a spacecraft comes out. Some spacecraft circle Earth. Others are carried deeper into space by more powerful rockets.

Apollo spacecraft

Saturn V
Height: 365 feet
Carried Apollo spacecraft and astronauts to the Moon between 1969 and 1972

All kinds of rocket

Every spacecraft and satellite sent into space has been carried there by a rocket. The first rockets were quite small and could only lift a small weight. So the first spacecraft and satellites had to be small, too. As people learned more about how to make rockets and how to launch them, the rockets became bigger and more powerful. Bigger rockets can launch bigger spacecraft.

The biggest rocket ever built was the American Saturn V Moon rocket. (The "V" stands for "5.")

Ariane 4
Height: 175–190 feet
Since 1981, Ariane rockets have launched more than 100 satellites from French Guiana in South America

Vostok spacecraft

A-class
Height: 110 feet
Carried the first Russian satellite into space in 1957, also the first living creature (a dog called Laika), in 1957 and in 1961, the first human being—Yuri Gagarin

Mercury spacecraft

Redstone
Height: 80 feet
Carried the Mercury spacecraft and the first American astronauts into space in 1961

10

Rockets like the Ariane have three stages. When each stage has used up its fuel, it is dropped to make the rocket lighter. Extra rockets, called boosters, can be added to Ariane to make it more powerful.

Second stage

Third stage

Nose of rocket opens, then falls away

Satellite's panels open in space

Rocket mission

Flames burst from the rocket's engines as it slowly rises off the launch pad into space. The booster rockets quickly burn up their fuel and fall away. The first stage falls away when it has used up its fuel, and engines in the second stage fire to carry the rocket farther into space. The second stage falls away next, then the third stage takes over. Finally, the rocket's nose opens, and the satellite is launched.

First stage

Booster rocket

Going to the Moon

In July 1969, millions of people all over the world turned on their television sets at the same time. They were watching something that had never ever been seen before—an astronaut climbing out of a spacecraft that had just landed on the Moon. It was the first time that anyone from Earth had walked on another world.

◀ When the astronaut Neil Armstrong stepped onto the dusty surface of the Moon, he was farther away from home than any other explorer had ever been.

Moon Buggy

On later Moon missions, astronauts took a special car to the Moon called a Lunar Rover, or Moon Buggy. It helped them get around the Moon's rocky surface more easily.

Service Module
Carried supplies such as fuel and oxygen

Command Module
Apollo's control center and living quarters

Lunar Module
Landed on the Moon

The Moon is our closest neighbor in space, but it is still 239,000 miles away. Altogether, 27 astronauts have flown to the Moon, and 12 have landed on its dusty, rocky surface.

Apollo spacecraft

The Apollo spacecraft was made up of three parts, called modules. The Lunar Module was the only part of the spacecraft that landed on the Moon. The Command Module was the only part that came back to Earth. The spacecraft had to carry everything the astronauts needed for their mission—including the air they breathed.

Apollo Moon mission

◀ Flames shot from the five engines at the bottom of the huge Saturn V rocket. Then it slowly rose off the launch pad and climbed into the sky. The deafening roar from its engines made the ground shake.

❷ Three hours after takeoff, the Command and Service Modules separated from the Saturn V rocket. They turned around and joined with the Lunar Module.

3 The Apollo spacecraft then went on into space. It took three days for the astronauts to travel to the Moon.

4 Two astronauts floated down a tunnel into the Lunar Module and flew it to the Moon. The third stayed in the Command Module.

5 The astronauts explored the Moon's surface and collected rocks. They also raised the American flag. There is no breeze on the Moon, so the flag was held open by a stiff wire. The flag—and the astronauts' footprints—are still on the Moon.

Moon rocks

6 To leave the Moon, the Lunar Module split in two. Its top half blasted off, using the bottom as a launch pad.

7 The Lunar Module linked with the Command Module. It was then cut loose because it wasn't needed any more.

8 The Command Module separated from the Service Module. It glowed brightly in the sky as it entered the air around Earth. Parachutes opened to slow it down before it splashed into the sea. The crew was soon picked up by a waiting ship.

Shuttle power

Most rockets and spacecraft are used only once. This is an incredibly expensive way of sending machines and people into space— no one would build a jumbo jet and throw it away after only one flight. A rocket-powered spacecraft called a space shuttle is different because it can be used over and over again. It blasts off from a launch pad like a rocket, but lands on a runway like an airplane.

Space junk

Space junk is a serious problem for astronauts working in space. Parts of old rockets and broken satellites still orbit Earth. If they collide, the fuel inside them may explode, sending pieces of metal flying in all directions.

Astronauts weigh nothing in space. When they leave their spacecraft, they have to clip themselves to it so they don't float away. This astronaut is repairing a broken satellite. His feet are safely clipped to the space shuttle's long robot arm.

The space shuttle

The shuttle is one of the most complicated machines ever built. There is nothing else like it. It can fly in the air like an aircraft and also in space like a rocket.

Booster rocket

Satellite

Robot arm helps move satellites

Flight deck

Orbiter

The main part of the shuttle is a spacecraft with wings, called the orbiter. It is carried into space by three large rocket engines and two booster rockets.

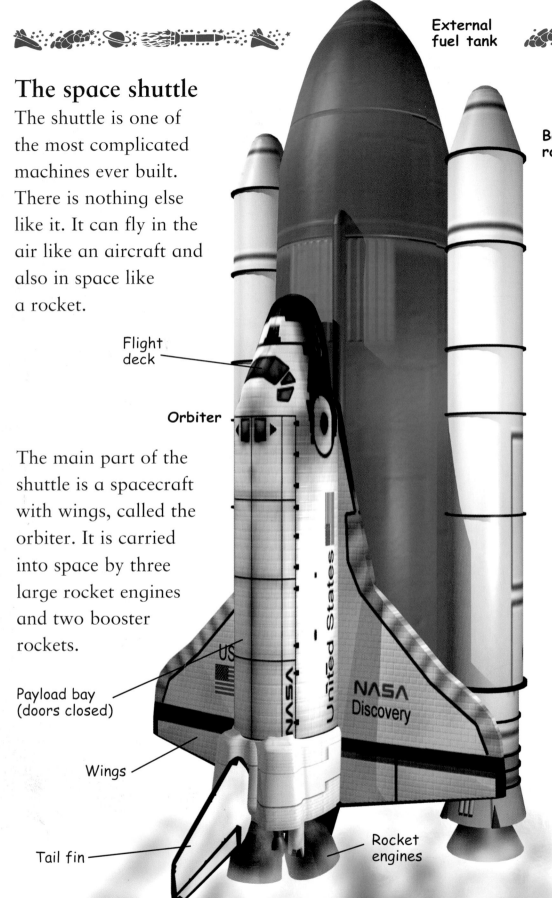

Payload bay (doors open)

Payload bay (doors closed)

Wings

Tail fin

Rocket engines

The space shuttle carries satellites into space in its payload bay. Sometimes it brings broken satellites back to Earth for repair. On some missions, it carries a laboratory called the Spacelab, in which scientists do experiments in space.

In orbit

Doors open and satellite is launched

Doors close

Fuel tank falls away

Shuttle mission

The space shuttle soars into the sky from its launch pad. The booster rockets and the external fuel tank fall away when they have used up all their fuel.

In space, the astronauts launch a satellite with the help of the orbiter's long robot arm.

At the end of the mission, the orbiter's rocket engines fire to slow it down, and it begins to fall back to Earth. It glows with heat as it plunges back into the air around Earth. Then it glides down and lands on a runway like a plane.

Rockets fire

Reenters Earth's atmosphere

Booster rockets fall away

Shuttle takes off

Boosters parachute into the sea and are used again

Glides back to Earth

Space suits

In space there is no air. Anything the Sun shines on is boiling hot, and anything in the shade is freezing cold. Human beings cannot live in space. We need air to breathe, and we need to be at the right temperature—not too hot and not too cold.

A spacecraft has to provide astronauts with air to breathe, and it has to keep them warm. When astronauts leave the spacecraft, they must wear a space suit, which does the same job.

Gas thruster

Adjustable arm

Hand controller

Nitrogen gas tank

Gas thruster

Manned Maneuvering Unit (MMU) helps astronauts fly around outside the shuttle

TV camera

Life-support backpack

Putting on a space suit

This space suit is called the space shuttle EMU, which is short for Extravehicular Mobility Unit. The suit has a special backpack that keeps fresh air flowing through the suit.

Parts of a space suit

All the parts of a space suit lock together at the neck, waist, wrists, and ankles, so the air inside cannot escape.

Gloves

Helmet

Top

Control panel

Radio headset

Underwear

Legs

Boots

The long underwear is covered with thin plastic tubes that contain water. Heating or cooling the water keeps the astronaut at the right temperature.

Life-support backpack

Working in space

Every day's work on board the space shuttle is set out in the flight plan for the mission. A typical mission may take ten days.

▶ In space, everything and everyone in the shuttle is weightless. So if an astronaut drops a pen, it doesn't fall to the ground. It simply floats in the air.

Strawberries

Vanilla pudding

Lemonade

Vegetables

Potatoes

Beefsteak

▶ Sleeping bags are stuck to the cabin walls so they don't float around. The astronauts wear a mask to block out the light. They are woken by music, beamed up from Earth.

▲ Shuttle astronauts have about 100 different kinds of food to choose from. Some food is dried and has to be mixed with water. Drinks are sucked through tubes so drops of liquid don't float around the cabin.

Space shuttle toilet

◀ Astronauts have to clip themselves to the seat when they use the toilet, or they might float away.

The shuttle carries up to seven people. The commander, in the left seat, is in charge of the spacecraft. The pilot helps the commander.

Mission specialists are trained to do a particular job on the mission, such as launching a satellite.

The commander, pilot, and mission specialists are all astronauts. Extra crew members, called payload specialists, are not. They may be scientists or doctors who do experiments in the Spacelab, or engineers who operate special equipment.

Eyes in space

A satellite floats silently in space, its camera pointing at the swirling clouds of a violent hurricane far below. Weather satellites watch the Earth and its weather all day and night. Other satellites beam telephone calls and television programs all over the world. There are hundreds of satellites orbiting Earth. They have become so important, it is difficult to imagine our world without them.

Navigational satellite

Weather satellite

▲ Even though they are far away in space, weather satellites can measure the temperature of the land and sea, the speed of the wind, and even the height of waves.

Navigational satellites allow sailors and pilots to check exactly where they are and make sure that they are traveling in the right direction.

Scientific satellite

Geostationary orbit

Satellite

Earth

22,375 miles

Some scientific satellites study the Earth. Others study the stars and planets and the space between them to help scientists understand how the Universe works.

Satellites in orbit

Communications satellites and weather satellites are often placed in a special orbit called a geostationary orbit. This means that they travel around the Earth at the same speed as the Earth turns, so they always point at the same part of Earth.

Communications satellite

Communications satellites allow us to talk to someone on the other side of the world just as easily as someone in the next street.

The Hubble Telescope

Stars look so beautiful because they twinkle like diamonds, but twinkling makes it difficult for astronomers to see them clearly through a telescope. Twinkling is caused by swirling streams of warm and cold air around the Earth bending the starlight this way and that.

A telescope in space has the best view of the stars because there is no air in space to make them twinkle. The biggest telescope in space is the Hubble Space Telescope, which was launched from a space shuttle in 1990.

Repairing the Hubble

When the Hubble was launched, astronomers discovered that its view was blurred because it had a faulty mirror. Shuttle astronauts mended the telescope in 1993. Since then, the Hubble has been sending clear pictures back to Earth.

Before repair

After repair

▶ The Hubble has two large, flat solar panels—one on each side. They make electricity from sunlight to power the Hubble's instruments. It sends its pictures to Earth by radio.

Space probes

Every 175 years, the giant planets Jupiter, Saturn, Uranus, and Neptune line up. This means a spacecraft can visit all of them in one trip. Two space probes, Voyagers 1 and 2, traveled all the way to these planets. They sent back some of the most beautiful pictures we have ever seen—of stormy orange and white clouds over Jupiter, volcanoes erupting on Jupiter's moons, and the broad, flat rings around Saturn.

Journey to the stars

Tiny space probes—some no bigger than a shoebox—have visited every planet in the Solar System except Pluto. A few have even left the Solar System altogether. Pioneer 10 is the farthest away. Since it was launched in 1972, it has traveled more than six trillion miles from Earth. It will not reach another star for eight million years!

Mariner

Mariner 9 orbited Mars in 1971, and Mariner 10 visited Venus and Mercury in 1974.

▲ The Voyager probes carry discs with pictures and sounds from Earth in case they are found by beings from another world.

Viking

Two Viking spacecraft landed on Mars in 1976 and tested the soil for signs of life.

Magellan

The Magellan space probe visited Venus in 1989. Its instruments made a map of Venus's surface.

Galileo

Galileo plunged into the gases surrounding Jupiter in 1995, sending information about them back to Earth.

Space stations

In the future, astronauts will visit the planets. Perhaps people will even live on Mars. But before this can happen, engineers need to learn how to build spacecraft for flights lasting years instead of days or weeks, and scientists need to study how very long spaceflights affect astronauts. The first step is to build a large space station in orbit around Earth.

Space Station Freedom

A new international space station will be built over the next few years. It will be home to teams of scientists and engineers who will learn how to live and work in space.